Wild Animals

by Jill Legaarden

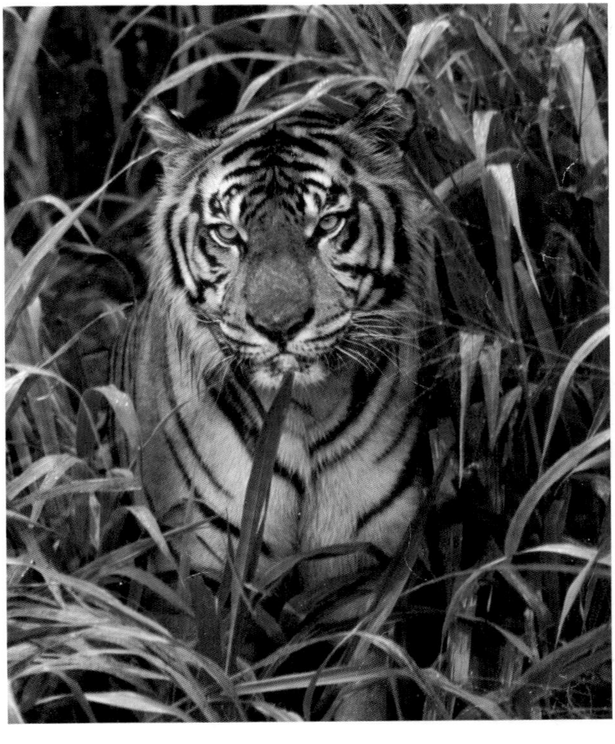

Scholastic Canada Ltd.

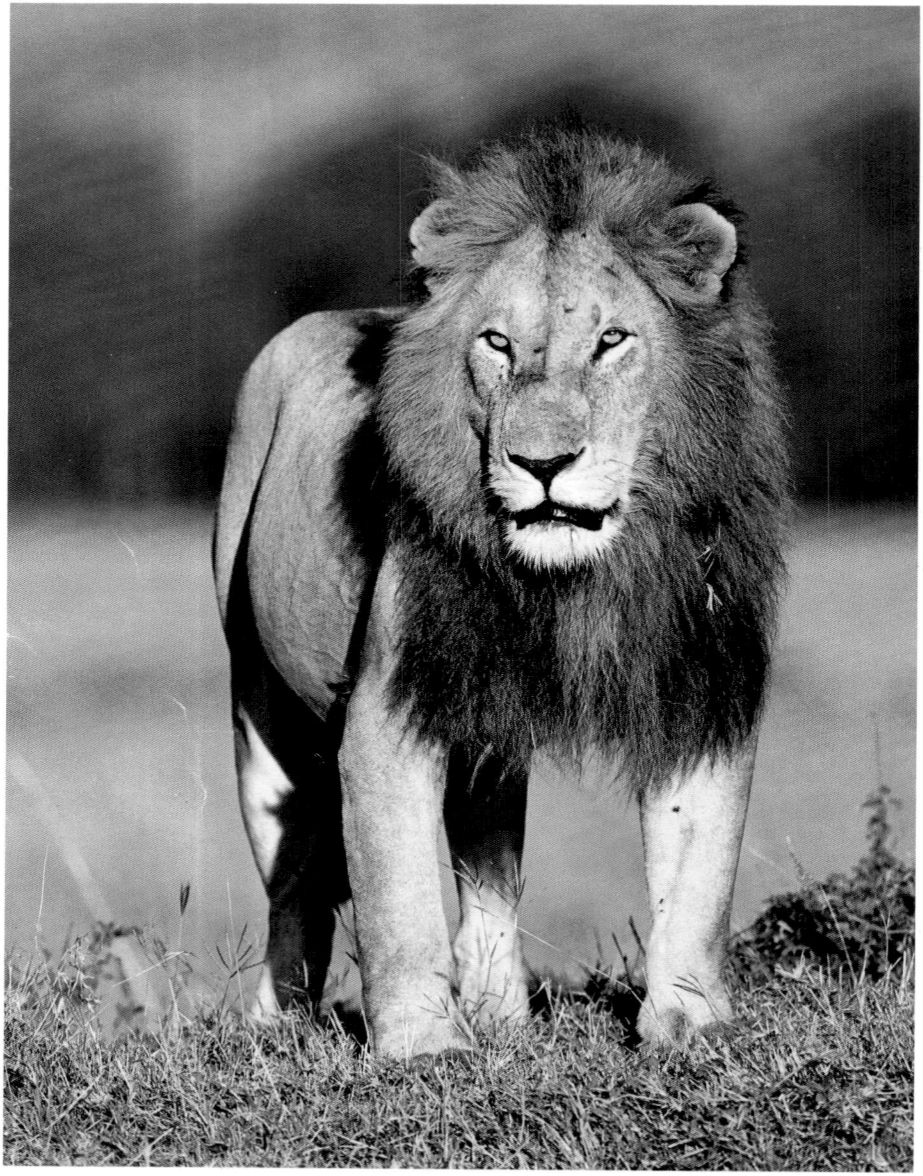

I see a lion.

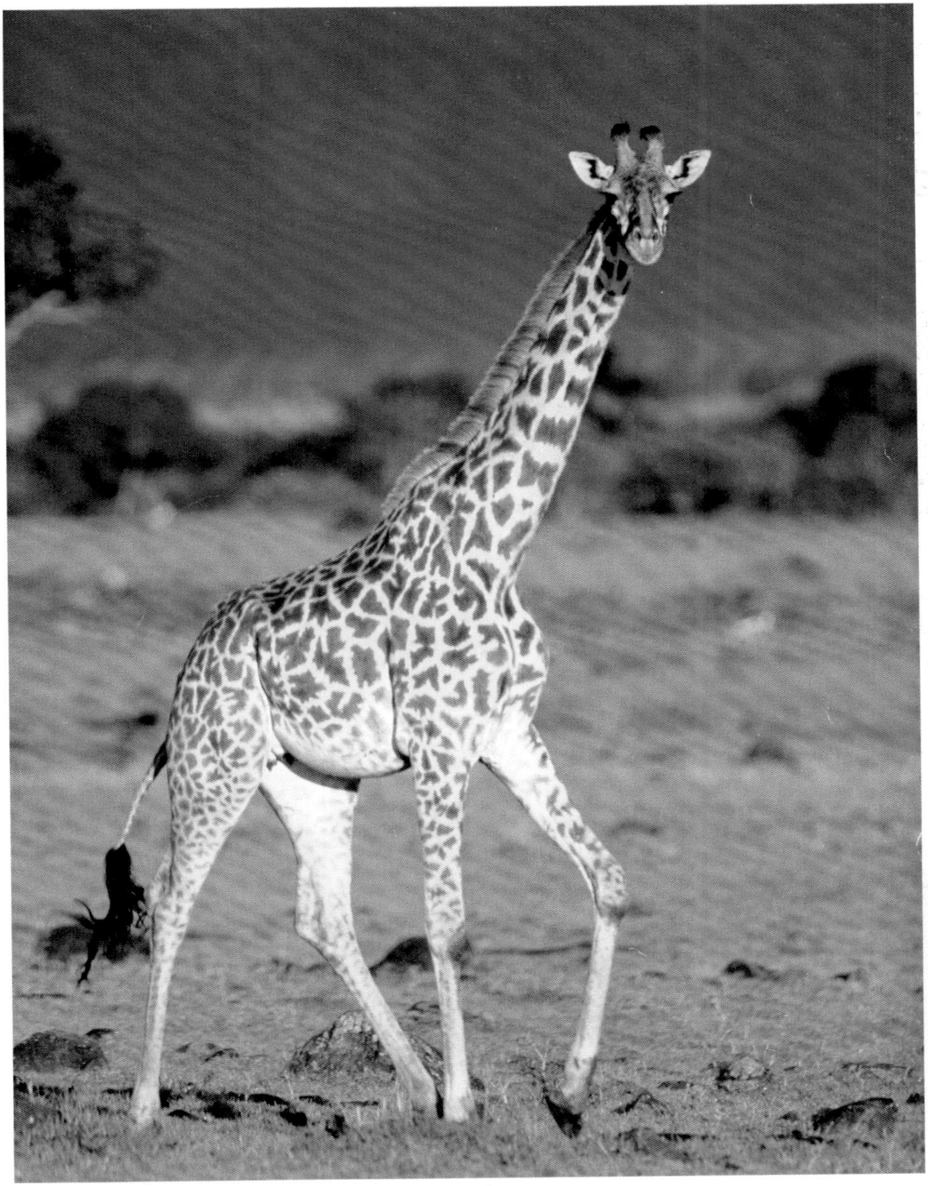

I see a giraffe.

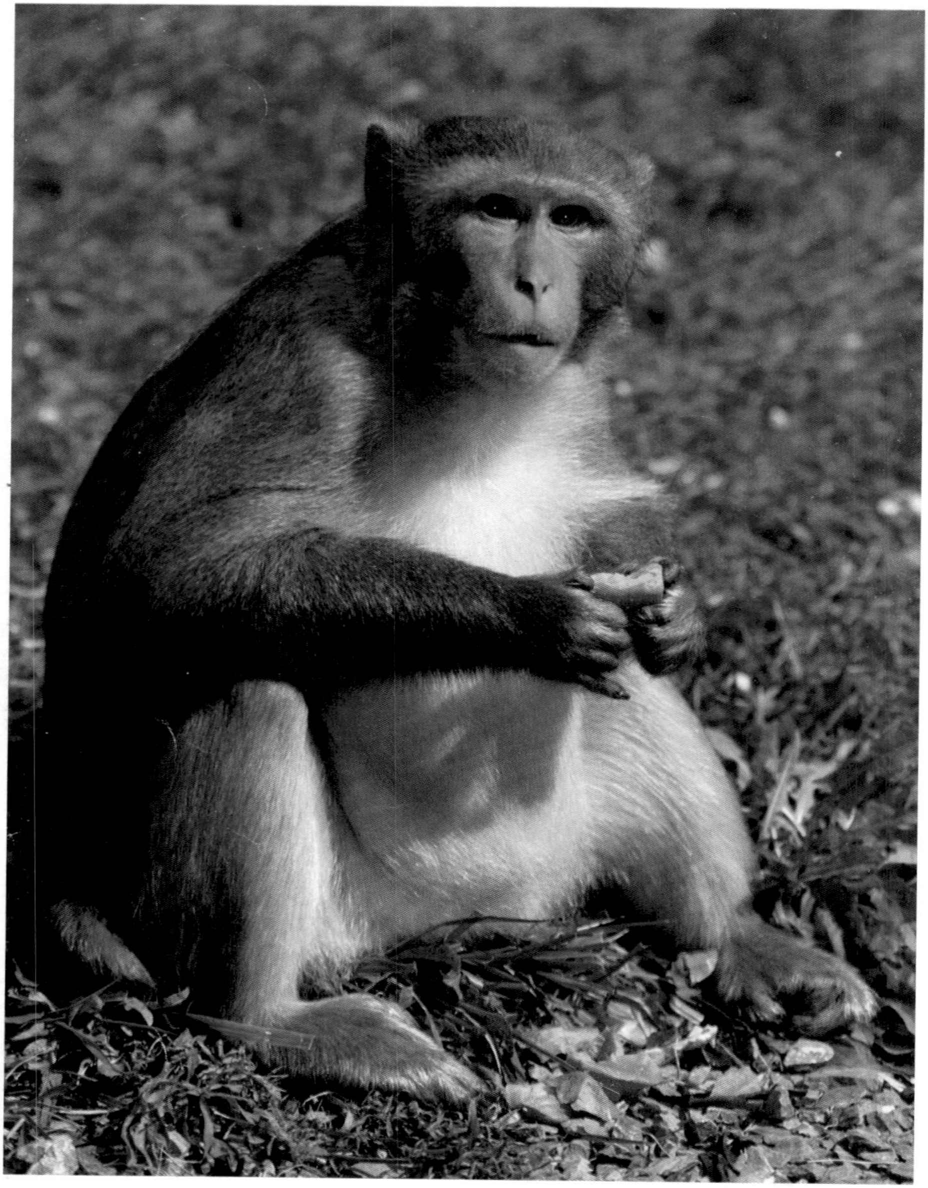

I see a monkey.

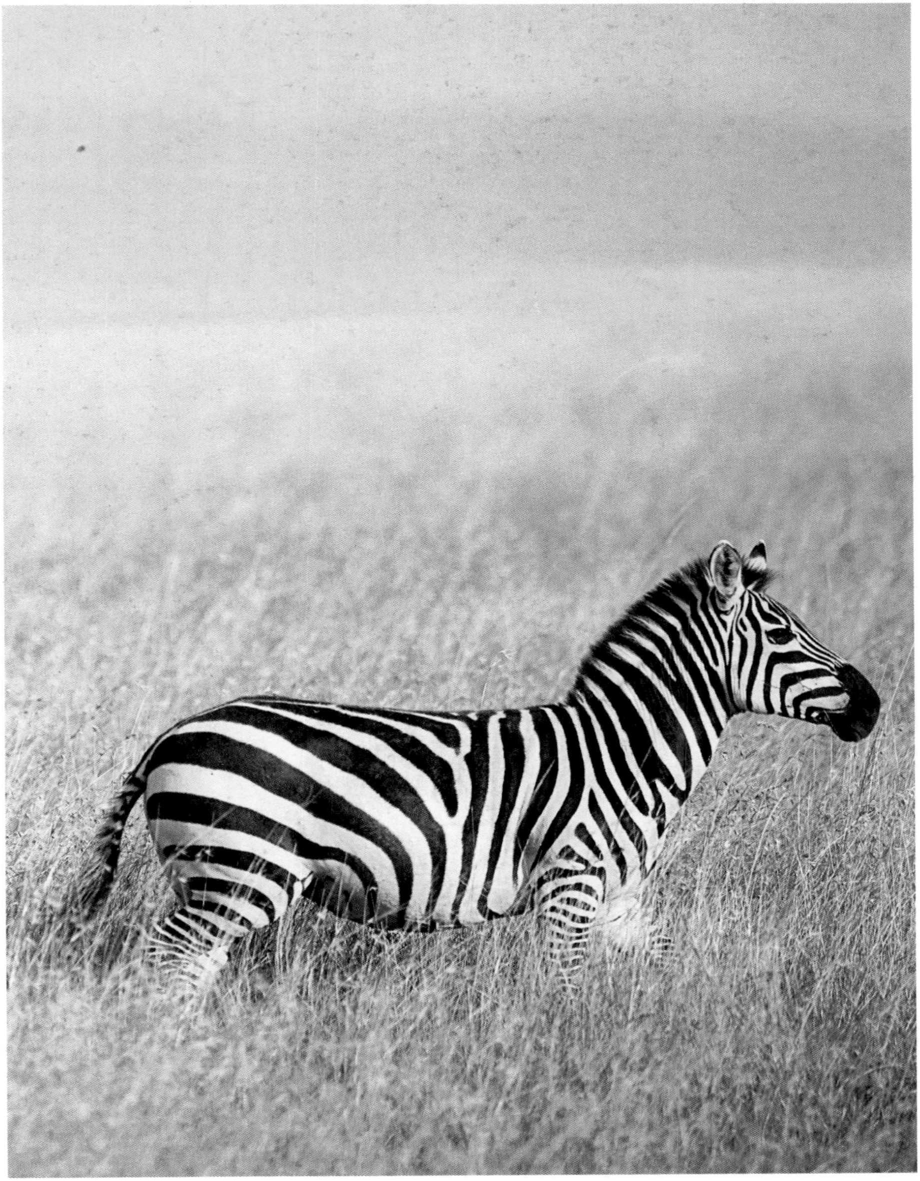

I see a zebra.

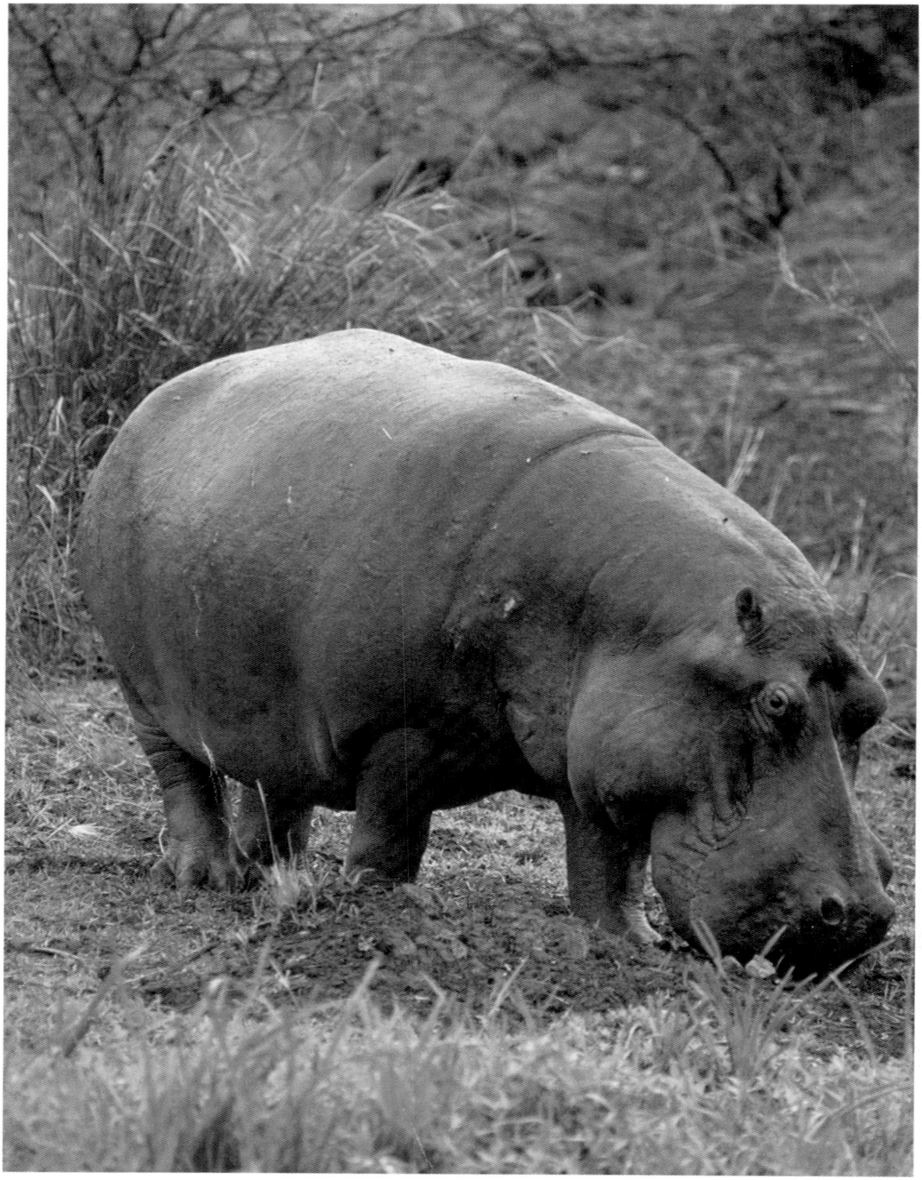

I see a hippopotamus.

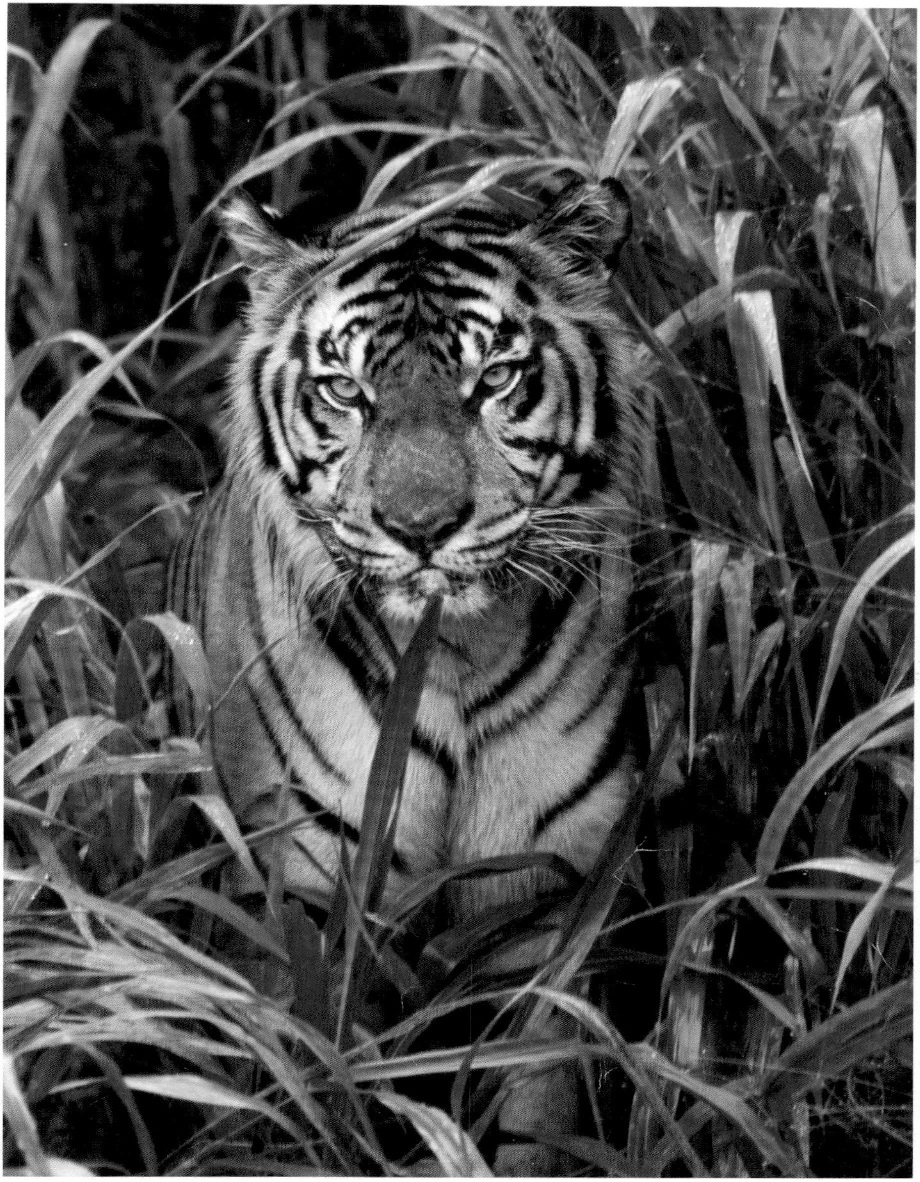

I see a tiger.

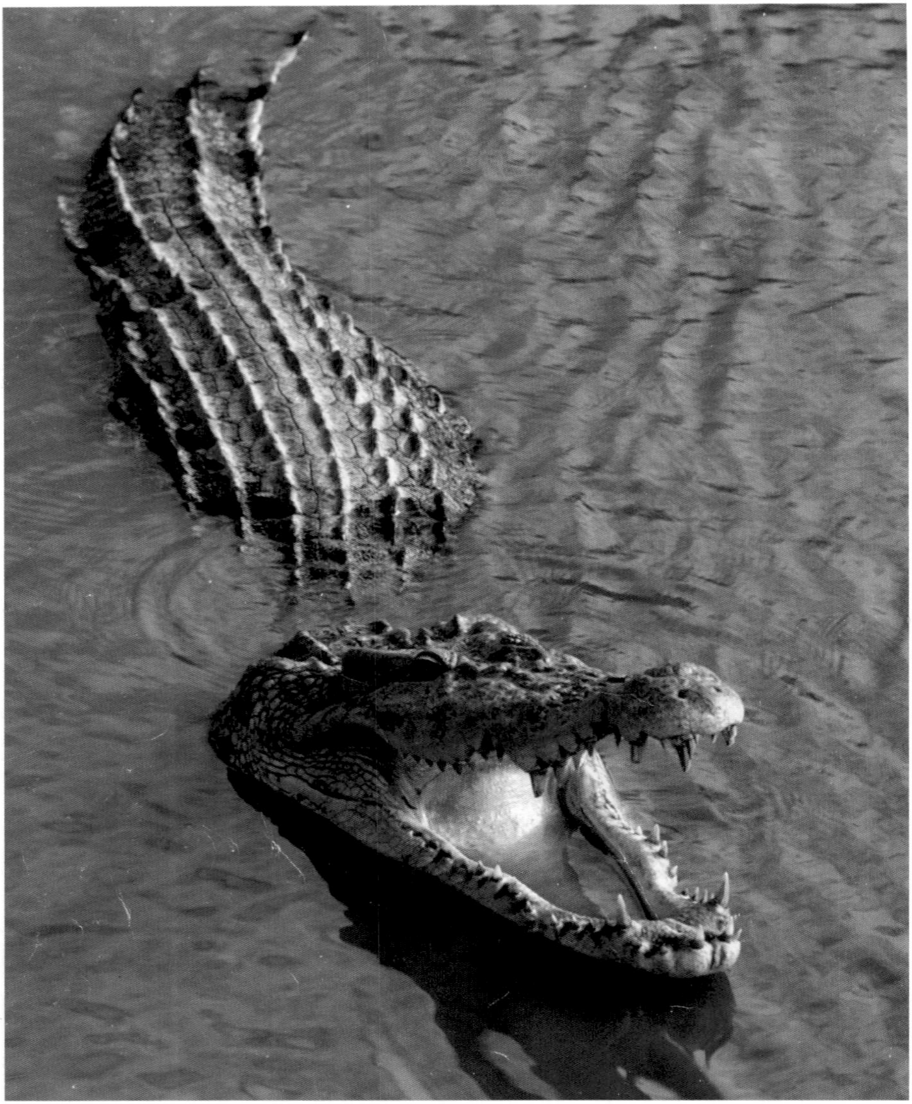

I see a crocodile.
Eeeeeek!